ICE-BREAKING WITH AI

The Answers We All Need

ABHIJEET A. SHUKLA

INDIA · SINGAPORE · MALAYSIA

ISBN 979-8-89277-935-7

Review Comments

Computer literacy was the buzz word of 20th century and here comes AI literacy in 21st Millennium. Today one can't afford to be a computer illiterate, so is the case for AI literacy in the near future. This book, "Ice-Breaking with AI", conceived and lucidly written by AA. Shukla, will enable even the novice in computer world to get interested in AI and encouraged to move further with a sense of ease and comfort possibly to learn and use AI.

A must read for the people who want to know about AI.

– Dr. Mylswamy Annadurai
(The Moon Man of India)

Chairman, Aerospace Committee, SICCI,
Distinguished Scientist &
Former Director ISRO Satellite Centre,
Padma Shri 2016

"A mandatory read for non-techies to stay relevant in AI era"

– Professor Abhishek Srivastava,
Indian Institute of Management Visakhapatnam

Simple and nice presentation which gives insight of AI smartly. 'Ice-breaking with AI' is an indispensable reading and will surely enlighten everyone.

– Senior Scientist Balwinder K.,
DRDO, MOD India

Dedication

To my ever-motivating Papa and lovely Mom

Table of Contents

Review Note

Computer literacy was the buzz word of 20th century and here comes AI literacy in 21st Millennium. Today one can't afford to be a computer illiterate, so is the case for AI literacy in the near future. This book, "Ice-Breaking with AI", conceived and lucidly written by AA. Shukla, will enable even the novice in computer world to get interested in AI and encouraged to move further with a sense of ease and comfort possibly to learn and use AI.

A must read for the people who want to know about AI.

– Dr. Mylswamy Annadurai
(The Moon Man of India)

Chairman, Aerospace Committee, SICCI
Distinguished Scientist &
Former Director ISRO Satellite Centre,
Padma Shri 2016

Preface

Joy and excitement of self-driving cars to ease of access offered by intelligent facial detection technology, anxiety from intelligent traffic violation monitoring systems and fear of losing our jobs. The topic of Artificial Intelligence (AI) unleashes a pool of curiosity, mixed opinions and feelings in our brain.

AI is becoming mainstream faster than we thought and it has started to have multi-dimensional implications on our daily lives. Our surrounding physical-digital ecosystem is now rapidly getting crowded with jaw dropping AI applications. Some of these applications are working with our consent, some are even without, some are noticeable by us and some are hidden in plain sight unknown to us. To my humble observation it seems that by the year 2050, the world population could be categorized either as consumer of AI or victim of AI.

The purpose of this book is to demystify and contribute in the democratization of AI. By promoting

AI Literacy, it aims at enabling healthy adaptation of AI technologies among the citizens of the world.

This book is here to empower readers from all walks of life to develop purposeful understanding of Artificial Intelligence and embrace the future with AI.

Overview of the Book

The word AI triggers so many questions, emotions and doubts! All of a sudden the rush of countless Why, What, How starts clouding our mind with speculations about the future of humanity with AI.

This book is primarily designed to encourage the general readership of non-AI experts like most of us. It answers some of the thought provoking questions but will, I hope, bring different perspective to the specialists for the greater good of human kind.

Containing 21 chapters written in the simple words used in our day to day communication. This book reflects the sincere efforts to bridge the gap between spearheading experts of AI and millions of eager AI consumers from the general spectrum.

CHAPTER 1

Why AI Literacy is Important for Human Kind

Artificial Intelligence (AI) is rapidly changing the world as we know and it is becoming nearly impossible to be unaffected by this change. AI is already having a major impact on our lives and it's only going to become more prevalent in the years to come.

That's why it's becoming increasingly important for humans to learn about AI. By understanding how AI works, we can better understand its potential benefits and risks. And we can also start to develop the skills we need to work alongside AI in the future.

There are many reasons why humans should learn about AI. Here are just a few:

1. To stay ahead of the curve: AI is a rapidly growing field, and those who don't keep up will quickly be left behind. By learning about AI, we can stay ahead of the curve and ensure that we're not left behind by this new technology.

2. To understand its potential benefits and risks: AI has the potential to revolutionize many aspects of our lives, but it also has the potential to create new risks. By understanding AI, we can better understand how to use it for good and mitigate its risks.

3. To develop the skills we need to work alongside AI: AI is already being used in a wide variety of jobs, and this trend is only going to continue. By learning about AI, we can develop the skills we need to work alongside AI and thrive in the 21st-century workforce.

There are many ways to learn about AI and this book here is your first step towards AI literacy. No matter what stage of life you are at, it's important to start educating yourself about AI. The sooner you start learning about AI, the better prepared you'll be for the future. Few important advantages of understanding AI are shared here-

1. Understanding and Utilizing Technology: AI is becoming increasingly present in our daily

lives. From virtual assistants to self-driving cars, and even in the workplace, AI is a powerful technology that has the potential to improve our lives in many ways. Having AI literacy allows individuals to understand and utilize this technology effectively, making it easier to adapt to and integrate into our lives.

2. Employment and Job Opportunities: AI is revolutionizing industries and creating new job opportunities. However, these jobs require a certain level of AI literacy. In fact the 'World Economic Forum predicted that while AI may replace around 85 million jobs by 2025, it will also create approximately 97 million new roles'.[38]

We can observe the relevance of this prediction in the present time. Having AI literacy will make individuals more competitive in the job market and increase their employability in industries such as data science, robotics, and machine learning.

3. Ethical Considerations: AI raises important ethical concerns, such as bias, privacy, and transparency. AI literacy allows individuals to understand these issues and make informed decisions about the use and development of AI. It also enables them to engage in discussions and debates about

the ethical implications of AI, ensuring that it is developed and used responsibly.

4. Critical Thinking and Problem-Solving Skills: AI literacy involves understanding how AI systems work, how they make decisions, and how they can be improved. This requires critical thinking and problem-solving skills, which are essential for navigating an increasingly complex world. AI literacy also encourages individuals to think creatively and find innovative solutions to problems.

5. Effective Use of AI in Education: AI has the potential to transform education by personalizing learning and improving teaching methods. However, to fully utilize AI in education, teachers and students need to have a certain level of AI literacy. It will allow them to use AI tools effectively and understand how AI can enhance their learning experience.

6. Empowering Individuals: AI literacy empowers individuals to be active participants in the development and use of AI. It allows them to understand the potential of AI and how it can be used to solve real-world problems. This knowledge gives individuals a sense of control and agency over their future and the future of AI.

7. Adapting to a Changing World: AI is constantly evolving, and having AI literacy will enable individuals to keep up with the rapid pace of technological change. As AI becomes more prevalent in our daily lives, having AI literacy will be essential for individuals to adapt and thrive in a world where AI is an integral part of society.

In conclusion, AI literacy is crucial for the human race as it allows individuals to understand, utilize, and engage with AI in meaningful ways. It also equips them with the necessary skills to navigate a world where AI is becoming increasingly present, ensuring that they can adapt and thrive in a changing technological landscape.

CHAPTER 2

Why Should I Learn AI

AI is rapidly changing the way we work, live, and play. It is already used in a wide variety of applications which directly affects our lives. Learning AI brings new ways of thinking as well as it brings a different way of thinking about the present and future of the world. By learning AI, you can develop new skills and perspectives that can be applied to other areas of your life.

Here in the points below are a few motivating advantages to learn AI.

1. Huge demand: AI is one of the fastest-growing fields and is in high demand across various industries. Learning AI can open up numerous job opportunities in areas such as data science, machine learning, robotics, and more.

2. Automation: AI has the ability to automate tedious and repetitive tasks, allowing humans to focus on more complex and creative tasks. By learning AI, you can develop skills to build intelligent systems that can automate various processes and make our lives easier.

3. Advancements in technology: AI is constantly evolving and driving advancements in technology. By learning AI, you can stay updated with the latest technological developments and be at the forefront of innovation.

4. Enhance problem-solving skills: AI involves solving complex problems and finding efficient solutions. By learning AI, you can develop critical thinking and problem-solving skills that can be applied in various aspects of your life.

5. Diverse applications: AI has a wide range of applications, including healthcare, finance, transportation, education, and more. Learning AI can provide you with the skills to work in diverse industries and contribute to meaningful projects.

6. Future-proof career: With the increasing use of AI in various industries, it is clear that AI will play a significant role in the future. Learning AI can ensure that you have a future-

proof career and can adapt to the changing job market.

7. Higher salaries: Due to the high demand for AI professionals, they are often offered competitive salaries. Learning AI can lead to higher-paying job opportunities and financial stability.

8. Personal development: Learning AI involves learning new skills, techniques, and technologies. This can help you develop personally and professionally, improving your problem-solving abilities, critical thinking, and creativity.

9. Social impact: AI has the potential to solve some of the world's most pressing issues, such as climate change, poverty, and healthcare. By learning AI, you can contribute to creating a positive social impact and making a difference in the world.

10. Aware against crimes: Learning AI makes you prepared for any unforeseen attempts of crime, frauds and harassments, etc. It makes you safer and more future ready with digital technologies in the physical as well as cyber world.

11. Aware about your rights: The AI Global Surveillance (AIGS) Index 2019 states that 56 out of 176 countries used AI for surveillance for safe city platforms [48]. Hence it becomes more

important at an individual level to become AI Literate. By understanding even the basics of AI makes you aware about your rights as a citizen when it comes to law enforcement with the help of AI technologies.

12. Being an informed citizen: Understanding AI makes you a future ready citizen of the world. It also adds safety, security and pride not only to you but also to the society and your country at large.

Addition to above all I would add that, Learning AI can be a fun and exciting journey. Building intelligent systems and seeing them in action can be incredibly rewarding and fulfilling, making it a worthwhile skill to learn.

CHAPTER 3

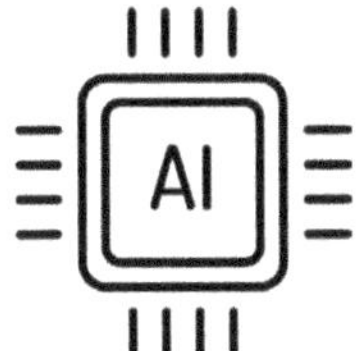

Introduction

Artificial Intelligence (AI) is a branch of computer science that focuses on creating intelligent machines that can think, learn, and adapt like humans. It aims to develop computer systems that can perform tasks that usually require human intelligence, such as problem-solving, decision-making, and understanding natural language.

The history of AI dates back to the 1950s, with the development of early computer programs that could play games like chess and checkers. Since then, AI has advanced significantly, and today, it is used in various industries, such as healthcare, finance, and automobiles.

There are various approaches to achieving AI, including symbolic AI, machine learning, and cognitive computing. Symbolic AI uses rules and logic to imitate human reasoning, while machine learning involves training computers with large amounts of data to make decisions and predictions. Cognitive computing combines these two approaches and aims to create systems that can understand and learn from data like humans do.

Some common applications of AI include speech recognition, natural language processing, image and pattern recognition, robotics, and virtual agents. AI is also used in predictive analytics, which helps businesses make informed decisions by analyzing data and identifying patterns.

While AI has numerous benefits, such as increasing efficiency and accuracy, there are also concerns about its potential impact on jobs and society. As AI continues to advance, it is essential to consider ethical implications and ensure responsible development and use of these intelligent systems.

In conclusion, AI is an exciting and rapidly evolving field that has the potential to revolutionize various industries and improve our daily lives. With ongoing research and advancements, we can expect to see more sophisticated and intelligent machines in the future.

CHAPTER 4

History of AI

Having experienced significant growth in the 20th and 21st centuries, AI or Artificial Intelligence, has a long history dating back to ancient times when it was described in myths and legends. However, it wasn't until the 1950s that it became a scientific field, thanks to the work of individuals such as Alan Turing and John McCarthy.

During this decade(1950s), the term "Artificial Intelligence" was coined by McCarthy, who organized the first AI conference in 1956. It brought together experts from various fields to discuss the potential of creating intelligent machines.

In the 1960s, the first AI programs were developed and the field experienced significant growth, with the creation of problem-solving techniques like the A* (A star) search algorithm and expert systems.

The 1970s saw a shift in focus towards specific areas like natural language processing and computer vision, but progress was slower than expected, leading to a decline in funding and interest, also known as the "AI winter."

In the 1980s, expert systems gained popularity but faced limitations, causing another decline in the field.

However, the 1990s saw a resurgence of interest in AI, fueled by the internet and advances in computing power. This decade also saw breakthroughs in speech and image recognition thanks to neural networks.

In the 2000s, AI continued to expand, with the development of machine learning algorithms and the use of big data. In 2011, IBM's Watson computer famously beat human champions on Jeopardy, showcasing the potential of AI.

The 2010s saw further integration of AI in daily life, with the rise of virtual personal assistants and self-driving cars. Deep learning also gained popularity and led to advancements in speech and image recognition.

Today, AI continues to evolve and face challenges, such as ethical concerns and its impact on society. Its future is uncertain, but it is clear that it will continue to grow and impact various industries and aspects of daily life, thanks to the continual rapid research and development.

CHAPTER 5

How Humans Created AI

Humans created AI through a combination of research, development, and technological advancements. The history of AI can be traced back to ancient civilizations, where humans first began to explore the concept of artificial beings and intelligence.

In the 1950s, computer scientists and researchers began to develop algorithms and programming languages that could mimic basic human reasoning. This laid the foundation for modern AI technology.

Throughout the 20th century, advancements in computing power and data storage allowed for more complex and sophisticated AI systems to be developed. Researchers also drew inspiration from fields such as neuroscience and psychology to better understand how the human brain processes information and makes decisions.

In the late 20th and early 21st centuries, breakthroughs in machine learning and deep learning algorithms have greatly advanced the capabilities of AI. These algorithms allow machines to learn from data and improve their performance over time, mimicking the way humans learn.

Another key factor in the creation of AI is the vast amount of data that is now (in 2000s and beyond) available. With the rise of the internet and the proliferation of digital devices, humans have generated an immense amount of data that can be used to train AI systems.

In recent years, the development of hardware specifically designed for AI, such as graphics processing units (GPUs), has also accelerated the growth of AI technology.

Furthermore, the collaboration between humans and machines has played a crucial role in the creation of AI. As AI systems become more advanced, they are increasingly being used to assist and augment human capabilities, leading to new breakthroughs and advancements in the field.

Overall, the creation of AI has been a collaborative effort between scientists, researchers, creative thinkers and technologists, driven by the desire to create machines that can perform tasks and make decisions like humans. While AI is still in its early stages, it continues to evolve and improve, with humans at the forefront of its development.

CHAPTER 6

How AI is Created

Artificial intelligence (AI) is created through a combination of computer programming, algorithms, and data. It is a complex process and involves expertise in one or many subjects as mentioned in the next chapter. However, we can simply understand the process of creating AI through the following steps:

1. Define the problem: The first step in creating AI is to identify the problem that needs to be solved. This could be anything from recognizing images to predicting stock prices.

2. Gather data: AI systems require a large amount of data to learn from. This data can come from various sources such as sensors, cameras, or databases.

3. Pre-process the data: Raw data is often messy and needs to be cleaned and pre-processed before it can be used to train an AI system. This involves tasks such as data formatting, removing duplicates, and handling missing data.

4. Choose an algorithm: There are various AI algorithms available, each designed for specific tasks. The choice of algorithm depends on the problem at hand and the type of data available.

5. Train the algorithm: The chosen algorithm is then fed the pre-processed data to train it. During the training process, the algorithm learns patterns and relationships within the data to make predictions or decisions.

6. Test and refine: Once the algorithm has been trained, it is tested on new data to evaluate its performance. If the results are not satisfactory, the algorithm is refined and re-trained until the desired outcome is achieved.

7. Implement in a real-world environment: After the algorithm has been trained and tested, it is deployed in a real-world environment where it can make decisions or predictions based on new data.

8. Continuous improvement: AI systems are constantly learning and adapting to new data.

This means they can continuously improve and become more accurate over time.

Overall, creating AI involves a combination of programming skills, data analysis, and problem-solving. It is a complex and iterative process that requires continual refinement and improvement to achieve optimal results.

CHAPTER 7

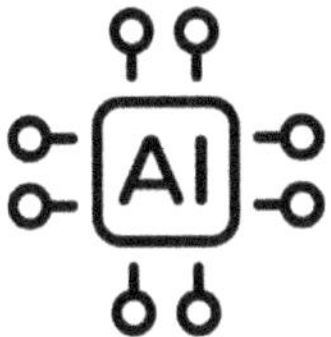

Foundations of AI

Foundations of AI (Artificial Intelligence) refer to the fundamental principles, theories, and concepts that form the basis of the field of AI. These foundational elements provide the framework for understanding and developing intelligent systems and algorithms.

Some of the key foundations of AI include:

1. Cognitive Science: AI draws heavily from the field of cognitive science, which studies the human mind and its processes. Understanding how humans think, learn, and make decisions is crucial in developing intelligent systems.

2. Computer Science: AI is a branch of computer science, and many of its foundations are based on computer science principles such as algorithms, data structures, and programming languages.

3. Mathematics and Statistics: AI involves complex mathematical and statistical models to process and analyze large amounts of data. Foundations in these fields are essential for developing AI algorithms and techniques.

4. Logic and Reasoning: Logical reasoning is a crucial aspect of AI, and it is used to construct intelligent systems that can make decisions and solve problems based on rules and constraints.

5. Machine Learning: Machine learning is a subset of AI that focuses on developing algorithms that can learn and improve from data without being explicitly programmed. This field has its own foundations, such as statistics, probability theory, and optimization.

6. Robotics: AI and robotics are closely related, and the foundations of robotics, such as mechanical engineering and control theory, are crucial for developing intelligent robotic systems.

7. Philosophy: AI raises ethical and philosophical questions about the nature of intelligence, consciousness, and the role of machines in society. The foundations of philosophy provide a framework for exploring and addressing these questions.

Overall, the foundations of AI are interdisciplinary, drawing from various fields such as computer science, mathematics, psychology, and philosophy. They provide the building blocks for creating intelligent systems that can mimic human intelligence and perform complex tasks.

CHAPTER 8

AI as a System

Artificial intelligence (AI) can be understood as a system or computer program that is designed to mimic human intelligence and perform tasks that normally require human cognitive abilities, such as learning, reasoning, problem-solving, and decision-making. As a system, AI consists of various components that work together to process information, make predictions, and take actions.

The key components of an AI system include:

1. Machine Learning: This is the process of programming machines to learn from data and make predictions or decisions without being explicitly programmed for each task. This is a subset of AI, it includes techniques such as deep learning, reinforcement learning, and natural language processing.

2. Natural Language Processing (NLP): This is the ability of a machine to understand and generate human language. This involves teaching machines to understand and process human languages. It involves techniques such as text analysis, speech recognition, and language translation.

3. Computer Vision: This is the ability of machines to interpret and understand visual information, such as images and videos. This allows machines to recognize objects, people, and other visual data. It involves techniques such as image recognition, object detection, and scene analysis

4. Robotics: This is the field of creating machines that can perform tasks autonomously, using sensors and algorithms to perceive and interact with their environment. This involves the use of robots to perform tasks that require physical interaction with the environment. It combines AI with engineering and computer science to design, build, and program robots.

5. Expert Systems: These are computer programs that use artificial intelligence to imitate the decision-making ability of a human expert in a specific domain, such as medical diagnosis or financial planning. These are AI systems that use knowledge and rules to provide advice or

make decisions for a specific context. They are often used in areas such as medicine, finance, and engineering.

6. Knowledge Representation: This is the process of organizing information and knowledge in a way that can be easily understood and processed by a computer. It includes methods such as logic, semantic networks, and ontologies. This also involves techniques for storing and organizing knowledge in a format that machines can process and use to make decisions.

7. Neural Networks: These are basically a set of algorithms inspired by the structure and function of the human brain. This uses interconnected nodes and layers to process information and learn from it. They are used in machine learning to recognize patterns and make predictions based on data.

8. Genetic Algorithms: These are algorithms inspired by the process of natural selection, used to solve complex problems by generating and evolving possible solutions.

9. Intelligent Agents: These are software programs that can act autonomously on behalf of a user or system, making decisions and taking actions to achieve a specific goal.

10. Deep Learning: This is a subset of machine learning that uses artificial neural networks with multiple layers to learn and make decisions from large amounts of data.

11. Problem-solving: AI systems use algorithms and heuristics to analyze data, make predictions, and solve complex problems. This involves breaking down a problem into smaller sub-problems, identifying possible solutions, and choosing the best one.

12. Planning and decision making: AI systems can make decisions and plan actions based on the available information and goals. This involves techniques such as decision trees, Bayesian networks, and game theory.

13. Natural intelligence: This is a branch of AI that aims to replicate human-like intelligence in machines. It involves researching and developing algorithms and systems that can think, learn, and adapt like humans. As human interaction is an implicit part of making any AI work in a reliable manner it also makes it the component of AI.

14. Inference engine: This component of an AI system is responsible for reasoning and making decisions based on the data and rules provided by the algorithms.

15. User interface: The user interface allows humans to interact with the AI system, providing input and receiving output in a way that is easy to understand and use.

Overall, an AI system combines several of these components to process data, learn, and make decisions in a way that is similar to human intelligence. The ultimate goal of AI is to create systems that can perform complex tasks and solve problems with a level of intelligence and efficiency that rivals or surpasses human capabilities.

CHAPTER 9

Types of AI

AI systems are classified and categorized according to their computational architecture, learning algorithms, and the problems they are designed to solve. These categories include:

1. Reactive Machines: These are the most basic types of AI systems that can only react to specific situations based on pre-programmed rules. They do not have the ability to form memories or use past experiences to inform future actions.

2. Limited Memory: These AI systems can use past experiences to inform future actions, but their memories are limited and they cannot learn from new experiences.

3. Theory of Mind: This type of AI has the ability to understand and infer the mental states of others,

such as thoughts, emotions, and intentions. It can use this understanding to predict and respond to human behavior.

4. Self-Aware: This is the most advanced type of AI that has the ability to not only understand its own existence but also have consciousness and emotions. It can think about its own thoughts and feelings and make decisions based on them.

5. General AI: Also known as strong AI, this type of AI has human-like intelligence and can perform any intellectual task that a human can. It has the ability to learn, adapt, and solve problems in any situation.

6. Narrow AI: Also known as weak AI, this type of AI is designed to perform a specific task or set of tasks. It is limited to the specific domain it is programmed for and cannot perform other tasks.

7. Artificial Superintelligence: This is a hypothetical type of AI that surpasses human intelligence and abilities in all areas. It is capable of solving complex problems and making decisions beyond human understanding.

8. Artificial General Intelligence (AGI): This type of AI is capable of understanding or learning

any intellectual task that a human being can. It is similar to strong AI, but not as advanced as artificial superintelligence.

The current stage of AI which has been achieved by humans is artificial narrow intelligence. Artificial narrow intelligence is a type of AI that is designed to perform a specific task or set of tasks. For example, there are AI systems that can beat humans at chess, translate languages, and diagnose medical conditions. Artificial narrow intelligence is not able to perform general intelligence tasks, such as learning from experience, reasoning about the world, and interacting with humans in a natural way. However, artificial narrow intelligence is still a powerful tool that can be used to solve a variety of problems.

Here are some examples of how AI is being used in the real world:

1. Chatbots are being used to provide customer service, answer questions, and even write creative content.

2. Facial recognition software is being used to identify people, track their movements, and even predict their emotions.

3. Self-driving cars are being tested on roads around the world, and they could eventually make driving safer and more efficient.

4. AI is also being used to develop new medical treatments, create new forms of art, and even design new products.

CHAPTER 10

How AI Works

Artificial intelligence works by mimicking human intelligence and decision-making processes using computer algorithms and data. It involves the use of machine learning, natural language processing, and other techniques to enable machines to learn, reason, and perform tasks without explicit instructions from humans.

The process of how AI works can be broken down into four main steps:

1. Data Collection: The first step in creating AI is to gather large amounts of data. This can be in the form of structured data (e.g. databases) or unstructured data (e.g. images, text, audio, video).

2. Data Preparation: Once the data is collected, it needs to be cleaned and prepared for use. This involves removing any irrelevant or noisy data and formatting it in a way that can be easily understood by the AI system.

3. Training: This is where the AI system learns from the prepared data. The data is fed into algorithms that allow the system to identify patterns and relationships between different data points. As the system is exposed to more data, it becomes more accurate and efficient in its decision-making.

4. Inference: Once the AI system has been trained, it can start making predictions and decisions based on new data that it has not encountered before. This is known as inference and is the core of how AI systems work. The system uses the patterns and relationships it has learned during training to make decisions or take actions.

5. Feedback and Improvement: AI systems continuously learn and improve through feedback. This can be in the form of user interactions, new data, or updates to the algorithms. As the system receives more feedback, it becomes more accurate and efficient in its decision-making.

6. Human Intervention: In some cases, human intervention may be necessary to correct errors or provide additional information to the AI system. This is especially important in cases where the system is dealing with sensitive or complex tasks.

One of the key features of AI is its ability to continuously learn and improve. As more data is fed into the system, it can adapt and make more accurate decisions. This makes AI systems highly useful in a wide range of applications, from self-driving cars to virtual assistants and medical diagnosis.

Overall, the functioning of AI involves a continuous loop of data collection, processing, training, decision-making, and improvement. The more data and feedback the system receives, the more it can learn and improve its performance. As AI technology advances, it is expected to become even more sophisticated and capable of performing complex tasks.

CHAPTER 11

How AI Learns

AI learning is the process by which an AI model is able to improve its performance on a given task by being exposed to new data and experiences. AI learns through a process called machine learning. This involves feeding large amounts of data into algorithms and allowing the AI to analyze and learn from the data. The more data the AI is given, the better it becomes at identifying patterns and making decisions or predictions.

There are three main types of machine learning: supervised, unsupervised, and reinforcement learning.

1. Supervised learning: This involves providing the AI with labeled data, where the desired output is already known. The AI then learns to identify patterns in the data and make accurate predictions based on those patterns.

2. Unsupervised learning: In this type of learning, the AI is given unlabeled data and is left to find patterns and relationships on its own. This can be useful for identifying hidden patterns in large datasets.

3. Reinforcement learning: This type of learning involves AI learning through trial and error. The AI is given a goal to achieve and is rewarded or penalized based on its actions. Over time, it learns which actions lead to the most rewards and adjusts its behavior accordingly.

In all cases, the AI continuously improves its performance by adjusting its algorithms and weights based on new data it receives. This process of learning and refining is similar to how humans learn, except that AI can process much larger amounts of data at a much faster rate. This allows AI to learn and improve at a much faster pace than humans.

Here are some examples of AI learning:

1. A self-driving car learns to navigate the roads by being exposed to new driving data continuously.

2. A spam filter learns to identify spam emails by being exposed to a set of labeled emails.

3. A natural language processing model learns to generate text by being exposed to a large corpus of text.

AI learning is a powerful tool that is being used to solve a wide variety of problems. As AI models become more sophisticated, AI learning will become an increasingly important part of our lives.

CHAPTER 12

Which Type of Problems Can AI Solve

As a powerful tool AI is capable of solving a variety of problems. Let's have a look at some of the most interesting ones-

1. Classification Problems: AI can be used to classify data into different categories based on specific criteria. This can be used in various fields such as image recognition, speech recognition, and natural language processing.

2. Prediction Problems: AI can be used to analyze data and make predictions about future outcomes. This can be useful in financial forecasting, marketing trends, and weather prediction.

3. Optimization Problems: AI can be used to optimize complex systems and processes by analyzing large amounts of data and finding the most efficient solutions. This can be applied in supply chain management, scheduling, and resource allocation.

4. Pattern Recognition: AI can be used to identify patterns and anomalies in large datasets that may not be easily identifiable by humans. This can be helpful in fraud detection, credit scoring, and medical diagnosis.

5. Decision-Making: AI can assist in decision-making by providing data-driven insights and recommendations. This can be used in business strategy, investment decisions, and risk management.

6. Natural Language Processing: AI can understand and process human language, enabling it to perform tasks such as text summarization, translation, and sentiment analysis.

7. Image and speech recognition: AI can identify and interpret visual and auditory information, enabling applications like facial recognition, object detection, and speech-to-text.

8. Robotics and automation: AI can be used to control and operate autonomous systems,

such as self-driving cars, drones, or industrial robots.

9. Fraud detection and cybersecurity: AI can detect patterns of fraudulent behavior and identify potential security threats in real-time.

10. Personalization and recommendation systems: AI can analyze user data and preferences to provide personalized recommendations and suggestions, such as in online shopping or streaming services.

11. Game playing: AI can be programmed to play games and compete against human players or other AI systems, such as in chess or video games.

Capability of AI to solve problems is just not limited to the above points. As new capabilities of AI are being developed rapidly every day the capabilities of AI are also varying.

CHAPTER 13

How AI and Humans are Similar

One of the most striking similarities between AI and humans is the ability to learn. AI systems can be trained on large datasets of data, and they can use this data to learn how to perform tasks. For example, AI systems can be trained to recognize objects in images, translate languages, and write different kinds of creative content.

Another similarity between AI and humans is the ability to reason. AI systems can use logic and reasoning to solve problems. For example, AI systems can be used to optimize traffic flows, diagnose medical conditions, and plan military operations.

AI systems can also be creative and imaginative. For example, AI systems can be used to generate music, art, and literature. AI systems can also be used to solve problems in new and innovative ways.

Some of the striking similarities between humans and AI are as follows-

1. Problem-solving abilities: Both AI and humans have the ability to analyze and solve complex problems by gathering and processing information.

2. Learning and adaptation: AI systems can learn and adapt from data, just like humans can learn from experience and adapt to new situations.

3. Decision-making: Both AI and humans can make decisions based on available information and weigh potential outcomes.

4. Emotions: While AI does not have emotions like humans do, some AI systems are designed to simulate emotions, such as chatbots and virtual assistants.

5. Communication: AI can communicate with humans through text or speech, just like humans communicate with each other.

6. Creativity: Although AI may not possess creativity in the same sense as humans, some AI systems have been developed to generate novel ideas and solutions.

7. Memory: Both AI and humans can store and retrieve information from memory to perform tasks.

8. Perception: AI systems can perceive and interpret sensory information, similar to how humans use their senses to understand the world around them.

9. Improvement over time: Both AI and humans can improve and become more efficient over time, with AI systems continuously learning and updating their algorithms.

10. Ethical considerations: Just like humans, AI systems also face ethical considerations, such as bias and privacy concerns, which need to be addressed in order to ensure fair and responsible use.

In addition to that, AI systems can also communicate and interact with people in a natural way. For example, AI systems can be used to provide customer service, chat with people online, and translate languages.

Despite these similarities, there are also some important differences between AI and humans. For example, AI systems are not yet able to experience emotions in the same way that humans do. AI systems also do not have the same level of common sense as humans.

Overall, AI is becoming increasingly similar to humans in many ways. As AI systems continue to develop, they are likely to become even more similar to humans in the future.

CHAPTER 14

How AI is Different Than Humans

Artificial intelligence (AI) is the simulation of human intelligence processes by machines, especially computer systems. AI research has been highly successful in developing effective techniques for solving a wide range of problems, from game playing to medical diagnosis. However, there are a number of important differences between AI and human intelligence.

One of the most important differences is that AI systems are typically programmed to follow a specific set of rules, while human intelligence is much more flexible and adaptable. This means that AI systems can be very good at solving problems that are well-defined and have a clear set of rules, but they can struggle to deal with problems that are more open-ended or ambiguous.

Another important difference is that AI systems typically lack the ability to learn from experience in the same way that humans do. This means that they can be very good at solving problems that they have been specifically trained for, but they may not be able to generalize their knowledge to new situations.

Some of the interesting differences which we can observe easily are as follows-

1. Processing Power: AI systems have significantly higher processing power compared to humans. They can perform complex calculations and analyze vast amounts of data at a much faster rate.

2. Memory Capacity: AI systems have a much larger memory capacity than humans. They can store and retrieve vast amounts of information without any degradation in performance.

3. Consistency: AI systems are designed to be consistent in their performance. They do not get tired or bored like humans, and can maintain the same level of accuracy and efficiency over long periods of time.

4. Objectivity: AI systems are not influenced by emotions, unlike humans. They make decisions

based on data and logic, which eliminates the risk of making subjective or irrational choices.

5. Ability to Multitask: AI systems are capable of multitasking and can perform several tasks simultaneously without any decline in performance. This is not possible for humans, who can only focus on one task at a time.

6. Learning Ability: AI systems can continuously learn and improve themselves through algorithms and data. They can adapt to new situations and make more accurate decisions over time.

7. Lack of Physical Limitations: Unlike humans, AI systems do not have physical limitations. They do not require breaks, sleep, or food, making them more efficient in completing tasks.

8. Repetitive Tasks: AI systems excel at performing repetitive and monotonous tasks, which humans may find tedious or boring. This allows humans to focus on more creative and complex tasks.

9. No Need for External Inputs: AI systems do not require external stimuli like humans do. They can function on their own, making decisions and taking actions based on their programming.

10. Ability to Process Unstructured Data: AI systems can analyze unstructured data such as images, videos, and natural language, which can be challenging for humans to process. This allows them to perform tasks that would be impossible for humans.

These are just some of the key differences between AI and human intelligence. As AI research and human evolution continues to progress, it is likely that at some point in future these differences may become less pronounced. However, it is important to be aware of the limitations of AI in order to understand its strengths and weaknesses.

So now we understand that AI systems typically lack the ability to understand the world in the same way that humans do. This means that they may not be able to understand the meaning of words or the significance of events. This can make it difficult for AI systems to interact with humans in a natural way or to perform tasks that require common sense knowledge.

CHAPTER 15

How Can I Learn to Work with AI

In a more conventional way, when we want to learn AI as a practitioner, the following points help in planning the approach to learn AI.

1. Understand the basics: Start by understanding the fundamentals of AI, including its definition, history, and various types of AI such as machine learning, natural language processing, and computer vision.

2. Learn programming languages: A good understanding of programming languages such as Python, R, and Java is essential for working with AI. These languages are commonly used in AI development and can help you create algorithms and models.

3. Take online courses: There are many online courses available that can help you learn the technical skills required for working with AI. Some of the best courses and material can be found easily over the internet for free.

4. Practice with real-world projects: The best way to learn is by doing. Look for opportunities to work on real-world AI projects, either through online platforms or by volunteering for projects in your community.

5. Join AI communities: Join online communities and forums where you can connect with other AI enthusiasts and experts. This can provide you with a platform to share ideas, ask questions, and learn from others.

6. Attend workshops and conferences: Attend workshops, conferences, and other events related to AI to keep yourself updated on the latest trends and developments in the field.

7. Read books and articles: There are many books and articles available on AI that can help you understand the concepts and techniques used in this field. Some of the books like "Artificial Intelligence: A Modern Approach" by Stuart Russell and Peter Norvig, and "Deep Learning" by Yoshua Bengio, Ian Goodfellow, and Aaron

Courville are effective resources for university level studies. However, you may refer to the bibliographical notes to get more credible reading resources based on your interest level.

8. Familiarize yourself with AI tools and platforms: There are many tools and platforms available for AI development, such as TensorFlow, PyTorch, and Keras. Familiarize yourself with these tools and learn how to use them effectively.

9. Network with professionals: Attend networking events and connect with professionals working in the field of AI. This can help you gain insights into the industry and potentially find mentors who can guide you in your learning journey.

AI is a constantly evolving field, so it's important to keep learning and experimenting with new techniques and technologies. Stay curious and be open to learning new things to stay up-to-date with the latest AI developments.

CHAPTER 16

How Non-Technical People Can Work with AI

As conventional learning may seem interesting to many technically sound readers it may repel most of us with little to no interest in math and coding. Hence in the following points there are some of the methods which may seem interesting and useful.

1. Understand the Basics of AI: While you don't need to have a deep technical understanding of AI, it is important to have a basic understanding of what AI is and how it works. This will help you communicate and collaborate effectively with technical teams.

2. Identify Business Problems that can be solved with AI: As a non-technical person, you can contribute by identifying business problems or

processes that can be improved using AI. This will help focus the efforts of the technical team and ensure that AI is applied in areas that will have the most impact.

3. Communicate Clearly: Effective communication is key when working with AI. Non-technical people should clearly communicate their ideas, requirements and expectations to the technical team. This will help ensure that the final AI solution meets the business needs.

4. Collaborate with Technical Teams: Collaboration between non-technical and technical teams is crucial for the success of any AI project. Non-technical people should work closely with technical teams to understand the capabilities and limitations of AI and provide feedback and suggestions.

5. Provide Domain Expertise: Non-technical people can provide valuable domain expertise to help guide the development of AI solutions. They can provide insights into the industry, business processes, and customer needs to ensure that the AI solution is relevant and effective.

6. Participate in Training and Education: To work effectively with AI, non-technical people should

invest in training and education to understand the latest developments and trends in AI. This will help them stay informed and contribute more effectively to AI projects.

7. Embrace Change and Continuous Learning: AI is constantly evolving, and non-technical people should be open to change and continuous learning. This will help them adapt to new technologies and tools and stay ahead in the rapidly advancing field of AI.

8. Use AI Tools and Platforms: There are many user-friendly AI tools and platforms available that do not require coding or technical expertise. Non-technical people can use these tools to automate processes, analyze data, and make informed decisions.

9. Stay Ethical: As AI becomes more prevalent, it is important to consider the ethical implications of its use. Non-technical people should be aware of ethical considerations and ensure that AI is used responsibly and ethically.

Lastly, non-technical people should stay updated on the latest advancements and applications offered by AI tools. It is also beneficial to experiment with demonstrative free software versions and keep an eye on the news related to AI policy and laws in the local territory. This will help in understanding how AI can be leveraged in their work and contribute to its development and implementation.

CHAPTER 17

What Can a Creative Person Do with AI

When it comes to what a creative person can do with AI, "imagination is the limit" is my answer. However, some of the interesting things one can start doing with AI are mentioned below to help start the imagination engine in our brains-

1. Create Art: Creative individuals can use AI tools to generate unique and innovative artworks. This can include creating digital paintings, sculptures, and even music compositions.

2. Write Stories: AI-powered writing tools can help creative writers come up with new story ideas, character development, and even dialogue. This can be especially useful for writer's block.

3. Design and Fashion: AI can assist fashion designers and graphic designers in creating new and unique designs. AI tools can help generate patterns, color combinations, and even clothing designs.

4. Film and Video Production: AI can be used in the post-production process of filmmaking and video production. It can help with special effects, color correction, and even generate virtual sets.

5. Advertising and Marketing: Creative individuals can use AI to create personalized and targeted advertising campaigns. AI tools can analyze consumer data and assist in creating effective and creative advertisements.

6. Game Development: AI can be used to create intelligent and dynamic characters in video games. It can also assist in level design and generating new gameplay experiences.

7. Virtual Reality and Augmented Reality: With the help of AI, creative individuals can develop immersive and interactive virtual and augmented reality experiences. This can include creating virtual worlds, characters, and interactive elements.

8. Music Production: AI-powered music composition tools can help musicians and composers create

new and unique music pieces. These tools can assist with melody creation, chord progressions, and even generate entire songs.

9. Interior Design: AI can be used to generate unique and personalized interior design ideas for homes and businesses. It can also assist in creating 3D models and virtual tours of spaces.

10. Writing and Design Assistance: AI tools can assist in proofreading, editing, and designing layouts for written content such as books, magazines, and websites. This can save creative individuals time and effort in the production process.

These applications are just a hint, and I am sure that by now several ideas have already come to your mind to try out with AI. You can use several free No-Code AI platforms over the internet to directly start working on them.

CHAPTER 18

How AI is Helpful in Creativity and Problem Solving

Artificial intelligence (AI) has been shown to be effective in a variety of creative problem-solving tasks. One example is the use of AI to generate new ideas. AI can be used to generate ideas by searching through a large database of information, identifying patterns, and making connections that a human would not be able to make. Another example is the use of AI to help with design. AI can be used to generate different design options, evaluate the feasibility of those options, and identify the best option.

Below are few of the interesting ways AI can help us in being more creative-

1. Generating new ideas: AI algorithms can analyze large amounts of data and generate new

ideas and solutions that humans may not have thought of. This can help in brainstorming and ideation processes, leading to more creative and innovative solutions.

2. Enhancing collaboration: AI tools can facilitate collaboration between different team members by providing a platform for sharing ideas and feedback. This can help in bringing together different perspectives and promoting creativity in problem-solving.

3. Improving efficiency: AI can automate routine tasks, freeing up time for humans to focus on more creative aspects of problem-solving. This can lead to more efficient use of time and resources, allowing for more creative solutions to be explored.

4. Identifying patterns and insights: AI can analyze large datasets and identify patterns and insights that humans may not have noticed. This can provide valuable information for problem-solving and can inspire new ideas and approaches.

5. Personalization: AI can analyze individual preferences and behaviors to personalize solutions and recommendations. This can help in tailoring solutions to specific problems

and individuals, leading to more effective and creative problem-solving.

6. Providing diverse perspectives: AI can be programmed with different perspectives and ways of thinking, which can help in expanding the range of ideas and solutions generated. This can promote creativity and out-of-the-box thinking in problem-solving.

7. Handling complex and tedious tasks: Some problems may be too complex or tedious for humans to solve efficiently. AI can handle these tasks and provide valuable insights and solutions, allowing humans to focus on more creative aspects of problem-solving.

8. Continual learning and improvement: AI algorithms can continually learn and improve based on feedback and outcomes, making them more effective in problem-solving over time. This can lead to more creative and efficient solutions being generated.

The use of AI in creative problem-solving is still in its early stages, but there is a great deal of potential for this technology. AI has the potential to help humans solve problems that have been difficult or impossible to solve in the past. This could lead to new innovations and breakthroughs in a variety of fields.

Here are some specific examples of how AI has been used to reflect creative problem solving capability:

In 2016 machine-generated art produced by Google's Deep Dream went to auction and proved its worth.

In 2017, IBM Watson helped a team of scientists develop a new drug to treat cancer. The drug was able to successfully treat cancer in patients who had not responded to other treatments.

In 2018, OpenAI created a new AI system called DALL-E that can generate images from text descriptions. DALL-E has been used to create images of everything from animals to landscapes to famous works of art.

These are just a few examples of the many ways that AI is being used to solve creative problems. As AI continues to develop, we can expect to see even more innovative methods and groundbreaking applications of this technology.

CHAPTER 19

What are the Key Skills to Co-Create with AI

There are a number of reasons why AI is well-suited for creative problem-solving. First, AI is able to process large amounts of information quickly and efficiently. This allows AI to generate a large number of ideas in a short amount of time. Second, AI is able to identify patterns and make connections that humans would not be able to make. This allows AI to find new and innovative solutions to problems. Third, AI is able to learn and adapt. This allows AI to improve its performance over time. These all capabilities of AI are here for us to utilize them, the following skills are helpful in being an effective user of this wonderful technology.

1. Communication: The ability to effectively communicate with AI systems, understand their

capabilities and limitations, and provide clear instructions.

2. Critical thinking: The ability to analyze and evaluate data and information provided by AI systems, and make informed decisions based on this analysis.

3. Creativity: The ability to think outside the box and come up with innovative solutions in collaboration with AI.

4. Adaptability: The ability to quickly adapt to changing circumstances and environments when working with AI, as their capabilities and requirements may change over time.

5. Problem-solving: The ability to identify and solve complex problems in collaboration with AI, using both human and machine intelligence.

6. Data literacy: The ability to understand and interpret data, and use it to inform decision-making and improve AI algorithms.

7. Emotional intelligence: The ability to understand and manage own emotions, as well as recognize and respond to emotions displayed by AI systems.

8. Technical knowledge: A basic understanding of AI technologies, algorithms, and programming

languages, to effectively collaborate with AI systems.

9. Teamwork: The ability to work collaboratively with AI systems, as well as other humans, to achieve a common goal.

10. Ethical awareness: The ability to consider the ethical implications of working with AI, and make decisions that align with ethical principles.

CHAPTER 20

Should We Fear AI

In today's rapidly advancing technological landscape, one of the most prominent and controversial topics is artificial intelligence. With each passing year, AI continues to evolve at an astonishing rate, raising questions and concerns about its impact on humanity. Even the creative industry like entertainment, design and art has been impacted, with artificial intelligence now being used to create, recommend and personalize content for users, such as images, paintings, movies and music.

While AI has undoubtedly brought about numerous advancements and conveniences, there is a growing sentiment among experts and individuals alike that humans should also harbor a healthy dose of fear towards AI. This sentiment stems from several factors, including the potential for job displacement, algorithmic bias, loss of essential skills, and the concentration of power and wealth in the hands of a few elites.

One of the most significant reasons why humans should fear AI is the potential for widespread job displacement. The integration of AI into various industries and sectors has the potential to automate many routine and repetitive tasks that are currently performed by humans. This could lead to significant job losses and a shift in the job market, leaving many individuals unemployed or struggling to find meaningful work.

Furthermore, AI has the potential to perpetuate algorithmic bias. With AI algorithms being programmed by humans, there is a real risk of bias being embedded into these systems. These biases can lead to discriminatory outcomes in areas such as hiring, lending, and criminal justice.

The loss of essential skills is another concern when it comes to AI. As humans become more reliant on AI for tasks and decision-making, there is a risk of losing certain essential skills. Creativity, critical thinking, problem-solving, and even basic human interaction skills could be diminished or forgotten as AI takes over these tasks.

Additionally, the concentration of power and wealth is a significant concern. As AI becomes more prevalent in society, those with access to and control over advanced AI technologies may gain unprecedented power and influence. This can lead to social and political inequalities, as wealth and power become concentrated in the hands of a few elites with powerful algorithms. These elites could potentially manipulate AI systems to further their own interests and agendas, exacerbating existing inequalities and marginalizing certain groups of people.

One potential consequence of the rapid advancement and widespread implementation of AI is the loss of human control. As AI becomes more autonomous and capable, there is a real possibility that humans could lose control over these systems. This loss of control raises concerns about the ethical implications and potential risks associated with AI. As AI systems become more sophisticated and autonomous, there is a potential for unintended consequences or even malicious use. For example, if an AI system is given the power to make decisions without proper oversight or guidelines, it could potentially make choices that are harmful or detrimental to humans.

As well as there are concerns regarding the performance and security of AI systems too. The opaque nature of AI algorithms makes it difficult for humans to understand and determine the accuracy or desirability of their outcomes. AI systems also pose vulnerability to security breaches and hacking, which could bring disastrous consequences if these systems are integrated into critical infrastructure such as energy or nuclear or financial systems.

However lucrative the promise of AI based growth seems, it is important for humans to proceed with caution, care, awareness and deep understanding of the potential dangers and risks associated with AI. Some of the best practices for sustainable adoption of AI include transparent and accountable algorithms, strict ethical guidelines, robust security measures, continuous monitoring and evaluation of AI systems, and ensuring human oversight in the decision making process with AI.

From a *different perspective*, concern of fear depends on the type and capabilities of AI being developed. Some experts believe that if AI is programmed ethically and with safeguards in place, it can bring great benefits to society. However, there are concerns about the potential misuse or unintended consequences of AI, particularly in areas such as job displacement, privacy, and autonomous weapons. It is important for society to carefully consider and regulate the development and use of AI to ensure it benefits humanity and does not pose a threat.

There is no one answer to this question as it depends on individual opinion and beliefs. Some people may argue that AI has the potential to bring about significant advancements and benefits to society, while others may believe that it poses a threat to humanity's safety and well-being. Ultimately, it is important for society to carefully consider the potential risks and benefits of AI and actively work towards responsible and ethical development and use of this technology.

CHAPTER 21

What is the Future of Humans with AI

Artificial intelligence (AI) is rapidly evolving and becoming more capable. As AI systems become more sophisticated, it is important to consider how they will interact with humans in the future. The future of the human race with AI is uncertain and constantly evolving. The coexistence of humans and artificial intelligent beings is a topic that has been explored in science fiction for decades, but it is only recently (in the past decade) that it has become a serious area of study. As AI technology continues to advance, it is becoming clear that we will need to find ways to live and work alongside these intelligent machines.

Some believe that AI has the potential to greatly benefit humanity by improving efficiency, increasing productivity, and solving complex problems. However, there are also concerns about the potential negative impacts of AI on society, such as job displacement, ethical issues, and loss of privacy.

Challenges will be there in finding sustainable and safe ways to integrate AI systems into our society. As AI becomes more powerful, it is likely to take on tasks that are currently performed by humans, such as customer service, data analysis, and even medical diagnosis. This could lead to job losses for some people, but it could also create new opportunities for others.

One possible future with AI is a symbiotic relationship i.e. AI systems will be used to augment human intelligence, where humans and AI work together to achieve greater success and advancement. This could involve AI assisting humans in various industries, such as healthcare, transportation, and finance, to make better decisions and carry out tasks more efficiently. AI could also help with scientific and technological advancements, potentially leading to breakthroughs in fields such as medicine and space exploration. This could lead to a more productive and efficient society.

One of the crucial challenges will be to ensure that AI systems are developed in a way that is safe and beneficial for humans. This means that they must be programmed with values that align with our own, and that they must be subject to the same laws and regulations as human beings.

Another possibility is that AI systems will eventually become so intelligent that they surpass human intelligence. This could lead to a situation where AI systems are in control of many aspects of our lives. This could have both positive and negative consequences. On the positive side, AI systems could be used to solve some of the world's most pressing problems, such as climate change and poverty. On the negative side, AI systems could also be used to oppress humans or even destroy humanity, leading to a future where AI becomes the dominant force. This could result in a loss of control and autonomy for humans, as well as potential conflicts between humans and AI.

It is not yet to predict but to prepare for what the future of AI will hold and bring for humans. However, it is important to start thinking about the potential implications of AI now. By considering how AI systems will interact with humans, we can help to shape a future where AI is used for good.

Here are some examples of how humans and AI are already coexisting in society:

1. AI systems are being used to help doctors diagnose diseases.

2. AI systems are being used to create art and music, such as GPT and DallE.

3. AI systems are being used to develop new drugs and treatments.

4. AI systems are being used to power self-driving cars.

These are just a few examples of how AI could be used to improve our lives. As AI systems continue to develop, it is likely that we will see even more examples of how humans and AI are coexisting in society. This could have a profound impact on the way we live our lives.

Ultimately, the future of the human race with AI will depend on how we choose to develop and use this technology. It will be important for society to carefully consider the ethical implications and ensure that AI is used for the betterment of humanity as a whole. It will also be crucial to continue investing in education and training to adapt to the changing job market and skills needed in a world where AI is prevalent.

Bibliographical Notes

Knowledge and understanding required to write a book comes from various sources. As an author the sources like books, online resources, own experiences, general contextual reading, interactions with various experts as well as GPTs, news, media, meditation, observation played an important role. Hence the bibliography of the book may exceed beyond and become too exhaustive to benefit, to keep it simple I am sharing some of the finest reads which I have found right to the time very interesting and rich in the context. I am hopeful that readers will also find this as an important resource to read deeper in the topics.

1. Artificial Intelligence: A Modern Approach – Stuart J. Russell & Peter Norvig

2. Life 3.0: Being Human in the Age of Artificial Intelligence – Max Tegmark

3. The Alignment Problem: Machine Learning and Human Values – Brian Christian

4. Human Compatible: Artificial Intelligence and the Problem of Control – Stuart Russell

5. Artificial Intelligence: A Guide for Thinking Humans – Melanie Mitchell

6. Artificial Intelligence by Example – Denis Rothman

7. Make Your Own Neural Work – Tariq Rashid

8. Hello World: Being Human in the Age of Algorithms – Hannah Fry

9. The Hundred-Page Machine Learning Book – Andriy Burkov

10. https://emeritus.org/blog/best-books-on-ai/

11. A World Without Work By Daniel Susskind

12. Genius Makers By Cade Metz

13. What Computers Still Can't Do By Hubert Dreyfus

14. The Alignment Problem By Brian Christian

15. Klara and the Sun By Kazuo Ishiguro

16. Rebooting AI By Gary Marcus and Ernest Davis

17. Four Futures By Peter Frase

18. Conversations with AI GPTs

19. https://www.forbes.com/sites/robtoews/2022/03/01/7-must-read-books-about-artificial-intelligence/?sh=1283b70546e9

20. Gödel, Escher, Bach: An Eternal Golden Braid (Douglas Hofstadter, 1979)

21. The Society of Mind (Marvin Minsky, 1986)

22. On Intelligence (Jeff Hawkins, 2004)

23. Alan Turing: The Enigma (Andrew Hodges, 1983)

24. The Singularity is Near (Ray Kurzweil, 2005)

25. Role exploration of Artificial Intelligence in Design Process, AA Shukla, IEEE ESAR International Conference 2019

26. https://www.forbes.com/sites/robtoews/2019/12/23/7-classic-books-to-deepen-your-understanding-of-artificial-intelligence/?sh=8e643821f6b9

27. Sustainable participation of Artificial Intelligence in design process, A Shukla Int. J. Adv. Res. Ideas Innov. Technol 5, 682-684

28. Descartes' Error: Emotion, Reason, and the Human Brain (Antonio Damasio, 1994)

29. The Mind's I (Douglas Hofstadter and Daniel Dennett, 1981)

30. https://oxfordsummercourses.com/articles/best-artificial-intelligence-books-to-read/

31. "Superintelligence: Paths, Dangers, Strategies" by Nick Bostrom

32. "Deep Learning" by Ian Goodfellow, Yoshua Bengio and Aaron Courville

33. "Artificial Intelligence for Humans" by Jeff Heaton

34. "AI Superpowers: China, Silicon Valley, and the New World Order" by Kai-Fu Lee

35. "How to Create a Mind: The Secret of Human Thought Revealed" by Ray Kurzweil

36. "The Master Algorithm: How the Quest for the Ultimate Learning Machine Will Remake Our World" by Pedro Domingos

37. https://newatlas.com/ai-art-film-writing-review/46891/

38. https://hrme.economictimes.indiatimes.com/news/industry/ibm-ai-will-necessitate-employees-to-reskill-in-the-next-3-years/102917251#:~:text=According%20to%20the%20World%20Economic%20Forum%20(WEF)%2C%20this%20evolution,its%20last%20five%2Dyear%20projection.

39. https://www.gartner.com/en/topics/artificial-intelligence

40. https://www.ibm.com/topics/artificial-intelligence#:~:text=Artificial%20intelligence%20leverages%20computers%20and,capabilities%20of%20the%20human%20mind

41. https://glenvleugels.medium.com/the-history-of-artificial-intelligence-51da64489b0

42. https://www.ncbi.nlm.nih.gov/pmc/articles/PMC9686179/pdf/ACTA-93-297.pdf

43. https://en.wikipedia.org/wiki/History_of_artificial_intelligence#Boom_1980%E2%80%931987

44. https://en.wikipedia.org/wiki/Timeline_of_artificial_intelligence#1950s

45. https://www.gartner.com/smarterwithgartner/top-trends-on-the-gartner-hype-cycle-for-artificial-intelligence-2019

46. https://teachonline.asu.edu/2021/12/gogy-galore-pedagogy-andragogy-heutagogy-course-design/#:~:text=With%20more%20faculty%20moving%20to,often%20presented%20as%20a%20continuum.

47. https://www.indiatimes.com/news/india/humanoid-sophia-makes-her-india-debut-in-a-saree-denies-marriage-proposal-from-a-facebook-user-336714.html

48. https://www.deloitte.com/global/en/Industries/government-public/perspectives/urban-future-with-a-purpose/surveillance-and-predictive-policing-through-ai.html

49. https://www.independent.co.uk/tech/sophia-robot-launch-hanson-b1792123.html

50. https://www.newindianexpress.com/cities/thiruvananthapuram/2022/jun/29/a-sophiasticated-date-at-cet-2470810.html

51. https://dl.acm.org/doi/fullHtml/10.1145/3491102.3517533

52. https://futureoflife.org/background/benefits-risks-of-artificial-intelligence/

About the Author

Known for his *different perspective* and unconventional innovation strategies, Abhijeet A. Shukla is an awarded and acknowledged Distinguished Design Researcher.

His versatile contribution to the field of User Experience and Design Thinking, *"the PSAV Design Methodology; an agile integration to the age-old design process,"* is extensively applied in both academic and industrial settings. He has authored some interesting research publications like '*Sustainable Participation of AI in Design Process*', and '*Role of AI in Design Process*'. He has co-authored '*Handbook of Sustainability in Additive Manufacturing*' and has created some valued intellectual properties in the form of design patent, copyrights and trademarks.

He holds a bouquet of interdisciplinary qualifications in Engineering, Design and Management from the prestigious institutions like IIT Kanpur and IIM Jammu. He is also a qualified Lawyer and critical to the effect of technologies and business practices on the social, economic and justice systems.